In the Beginning Was the Word

Teaching Reading & Writing Through The Bible

By Ruth J. Colvin

Literacy Volunteers of America, Inc.

All proceeds from the sale of this book go to further the work of LVA.

Production costs for this book were funded by grants from The John Ben Snow Foundation, Lewis-Trinity Fund, Ethel G. Salisbury, Virginia Simons, and other friends of LVA.

i

About Literacy Volunteers of America, Inc.

Literacy Volunteers of America, Inc. (LVA) is a nonprofit educational organization, founded in 1962, which trains volunteer tutors to teach adults and teens to read, write, understand, and speak English. By 1994, over a third of a million people had received help in these areas from LVA. A private voluntary organization, LVA receives funding through the sale of its training materials and services, contributions from individuals, corporations, foundations, and from special government projects. It is governed by a national volunteer Board of Directors. The state level and local level affiliates are organized and directed by volunteer Boards. LVA training materials are used by libraries, churches, correctional facilities, adult basic education, public school classes, colleges, and universities as well as by LVA affiliates.

For further information about Literacy Volunteers of America, Inc. contact:

LITERACY VOLUNTEERS OF AMERICA, INC.
5795 WIDEWATERS PARKWAY
SYRACUSE, NY 13214-1846

TELEPHONE: (315) 445-8000
FAX: (315) 445-8006

Printed in the United States of America.
ISBN 0-930713-59-1
LVA Order #50012

PRODUCTION EDITOR: Jeffrey Charboneau
DESIGNER: Laura Mason
COVER DESIGN/ILLUSTRATION: Annie Vallotton

To my students,
who have helped me grow
as we learned together.

Acknowledgments

I am constantly striving for a "balanced life" — physical, mental, emotional, undergirded by spiritual. My work in Literacy Volunteers demanded that balance.

There had to be the physical part, whether it was meeting my students, lifting boxes of books and records as offices were set up in various places, speaking to diversified groups in recruiting students, tutors, board and committee members. The mental factors were tapped in searching out new techniques of teaching, in learning how to work first with all volunteers and later with staff, and in learning how to simplify those sometimes difficult concepts. The emotional always was involved as I met and worked with so many fine, sensitive people who had not had opportunities to learn to read. But underneath it all was my spiritual beliefs, my firm faith that Someone continues to work with and through me, together with the work and commitment of the thousands of Literacy Volunteers, contributing to the success of Literacy Volunteers of America, Inc.

Without the willingness of students to experiment with me, to let me know of their wants and needs in reading and writing biblical material, this book would have been meaningless. I thank them as well as those other students whose stories I have shared.

My thanks go to those who reviewed the manuscript, some for accuracy of biblical references, other for clarity or writing, and still others for general readability and understanding — all giving helpful suggestions and comments: Rev. Eugene Turner, Dr. Kevin O'Connell, S.J., Rabbi Sheldon Ezring, Isabel Wolseley, Dr, Judy Cheatham, David Briddell, Dorothy Ortner, Clarence Jordon, Dr. Jodi Crandall and Harry Briley. Too, I thank the LVA trainers and practitioners for their suggestions: Kaye Beal, Bernice Cartrett, Joyia Culpepper, Pam Krenzke, Edith Lee, Gail Rice, Connie Schwein, Marsi Simpkins, and Betty Williford.

Special thanks to Annie Vallotton, artist for the *Good News Bible,* who generously shared her remarkable talents by giving illustrations to greatly enhance this book. And to Rev. Ted Taylor for letting me paraphrase his meaningful sermon, and to Joan Anglund for sharing her poem about teachers.

I hope other tutors and students will have as meaningful experiences as we did, that there will be joy in new friendships as you learn together.

Ruth J. Colvin

About the Author

*R*UTH COLVIN is the Founder and served as the first President of LVA. At present she is Chair of the Research and Development Committee and the International Committee. She continues to be active as a volunteer tutor in both Basic Reading and English as a Second Language — reaching out to adapt new methods to LVA's one-to-one and small group tutoring. She has served on many boards, always learning and sharing ideas.

Photo by Steve Sartori

Since 1962, Ruth and Bob Colvin have traveled all over the United States and the world giving Basic Reading and conversational English (ESL) tutor training workshops. The recipient of seven honorary Doctors of Humane Letters, Ruth was awarded the United States of America's President's Volunteer Action Award in 1987, the nation's highest award given to a volunteer. In 1993, she was inducted into the National Women's Hall of Fame.

Ruth and Bob have two children — a daughter, Lindy, and a son, Terry, and 6 grandchildren. She lives with husband Bob, in Syracuse, NY and is active in the Pebble Hill Presbyterian Church in DeWitt, NY.

Ruth is also coauthor or author of:

TUTOR, a handbook for literacy teachers

READ, an assessment tool for adult new readers

I Speak English, a handbook for teachers of conversational English

A Way With Words, the story of Literacy Volunteers of America

Contents

In the beginning
was the Word,
and the Word
was with God.

John 1:1
(New Revised Standard Version)

INTRODUCTION

I sat quietly in the back of a small inner-city church in Syracuse, NY, observing the worshippers dressed in their Sunday best. My husband, Bob, and I were the only white people in the church. Back in the early 1960s that wasn't unusual, for there was little integration even within the Christian community.

The assistant preacher of the Word of Hope Church had invited us to attend this Sunday morning. But, the parishioners didn't know that. They only saw that white strangers were among them, and they looked beyond us with silent stares.

The Reverend Frank Sampson walked slowly up to the pulpit, opened his large Bible, and read: "The Lord is my shepherd. I shall not want."

As he continued through the 23rd Psalm, I looked at him in astonishment. How could he read those difficult words? Frank was one of my early students in the Literacy Volunteers program, and I knew he couldn't read at all. He signed his name with an "X." He had never been to school a day in his life.

Frank was a man of perhaps 40, a dishwasher at a small diner and later a maintenance man at a local factory. He was married, with one son. Frank was a quiet man, honest, hard-working, and dedicated to his church and to God. Because of his long working hours, we usually held our tutoring sessions at 7 a.m. in the back of a grocery store, sitting on a bench, empty cardboard boxes stacked around us. Frank's greatest desire was to read the Bible.

As the service progressed, I began looking back through my own life. How had I learned the 23rd Psalm and the Lord's Prayer? I couldn't recall reading them until much later. Someone had taught me, and I had memorized them. That's how Frank "read" the Bible. He had heard the verses so often that he knew them by heart. He could open the Bible to any page; it made no difference which one. He "read" the passages he had memorized—those he wanted for his biblical text that day.

How then did Frank Sampson become a preacher? He couldn't have gone to study at what we think of as a regular seminary, for he was unable to read. Later I would come to learn that in some churches, formal education is not necessary. It is a spiritual experience where a man or woman is "called by God" to preach the gospel, and this call is recognized by a group of people who designate him as their pastor. Frank Sampson had received such a call.

Rev. Sampson was obviously a leader of his people. Is education a prerequisite to leadership? If we look to history, we find many inspired leaders with little or no formal education.

Frank thought his major deficiency was that he was unable to read or write. Could I help him? Back then, few people realized that illiteracy was a major problem in the United States. Little training was available to help me teach basic reading and writing. I did what I could, but we were both discouraged. I wish that I had possessed the knowledge and training I now have. There are so many ways I could have helped him learn to read what *he* wanted to read—so many ways I could have helped him get his thoughts on paper.

That experience remained in the back of my mind for many years. I knew that someday I had to do more research and get practical experience. Then I could apply my findings to someone else who also wanted to learn to read in order to read the Bible.

Over the years, I have worked one-to-one and in small-group settings, teaching and learning. During that time I have developed and adapted techniques to teach adults who want help in reading and writing specifically so they can read scriptures and biblical material, thus enabling them to participate more fully in their own religious activities.

For a long time I resisted addressing this issue, however, because I don't believe in proselytizing. I believe in teaching people to read so that they can make their own decisions. But Literacy Volunteers of America, Inc. (LVA) is learner-centered, and I finally realized I wasn't listening. I knew I had to do something. That "something" ended up being the creation of this book.

In the Beginning Was the Word: Teaching Reading and Writing Through the Bible has been written from a Christian perspective, but the techniques can easily be adapted to any religious material. Jewish resource materials are available from local synagogues, adapting the lessons to the Hebrew Scriptures. Similarly, the techniques and resource material used could be adapted to other religious books.

I use "students" and "learners" interchangeably, although I'm hesitant to say that the students are the only learners. We, as tutors, are learners as well. I refer to "tutors" and "students" in the plural because I am addressing this book to all tutors about all students, whether the setting is one-to-one or small groups. For ease of reading, I use *he* when referring to students and *she* when referring to tutors. The names of specific tutors and students that appear in this book have been changed to protect their privacy.

When God's children
are in need,
You be the one
to help them out.

Romans 12:13
(Bible for Students)

ADULTS WHO WANT
TO LEARN TO READ THE BIBLE

*"In the beginning God created the heavens
and the earth..."*

"The Lord is my shepherd, I shall not want..."

"Thou shalt have no other gods before me..."

"Our Father, who art in heaven..."

"Blessed are the poor in spirit..."

"For God so loved the world..."

These are passages from the Bible that are known, memorized, and repeated by numerous people—people who cannot read them. Thousands of people who have applied to Literacy Volunteers of America, Inc. (LVA) and other literacy and basic reading/writing programs for help have made reading the Bible a high priority for why they want to learn to read better.

People generally read more easily books or magazines of interest to them—what they want to know more about. So, when people have reading problems, why not focus on specific materials selected by the students themselves?

Thousands of Americans know their Bible—the stories, the parables, the Lord's Prayer, the Psalms. Many of these same Americans want to read the Bible for themselves, but can't. They want and need help. LVA recommends that learners choose their own study materials as they are taught reading and writing skills. For those who want knowledge of the Bible, why not utilize it as you teach?

Who are these adults? They are young and old, from 16 to 80 years of age, who want to improve specific skills so they can study the Bible. They reflect the general church-going population, coming from a variety of religious, economic, and ethnic backgrounds. But these learners go far beyond the traditional religious community.

In addition, there are many young people who are not included in religious church groups, but who are also looking inward. They resent being "told" what to believe or what not to believe. They want to read and find out for themselves.

WHY CAN'T THEY READ?

It's true that America has compulsory education, but it hasn't always been so. Not too many years ago many states were quite lax in their school attendance laws. Numerous youngsters of the 20s, 30s, 40s, and even 50s who are now in their middle or later lives, had little if any schooling.

Even today, a large percentage of young people "fall between the cracks." They get social promotions, skip too many days of school, or just sit quietly in over-crowded classes—some not so quietly—waiting until they are old enough to drop out.

Most of these adults who want help in reading the Bible have the same characteristics as other adults who have limited reading and writing skills. They're hesitant to admit their lack of formal schooling and their inability to read the Bible.

MOST ADULT LEARNERS:

- Are creative and adaptable
- Are apprehensive or anxious
- Learn unevenly
- Have outside responsibilities beyond tutoring sessions
- View themselves as responsible, self-directed, independent
- Prefer to make their own decisions
- Resent being treated like children
- Are threatened by formal tests [1]

Some of these adult learners have rich backgrounds in Christianity, Islam, and Judaism, being long-standing leaders in their places of worship. Many of them know most of the Bible stories, having taught Sunday School, Bible, or religious classes for years. Their frustration surfaces when they cannot *read* the texts or any other new material given to them. They must depend on their memories to recall stories they were told as children.

Others sing in church choirs. They have memorized the words as well as the music, and many of the hymns are old favorites they have known all their lives. But what happens when the choir leader gives out new music? Most are unwilling to admit in front of their peers that they cannot read the words of a new hymn. What do they do? They often look at the score and pretend, humming along. They wait patiently, trying to blend into the group, picking up the text as the choir sings the words again and again.

Then there are the parishioners: "It's rough when the preacher tells you what Scripture he's using on Sunday morning, and everybody else in the church looks it up," said one man. "You can't pretend 'cause you'd be sure to get the wrong page and you shouldn't just sit there 'cause you'd look like you didn't care." [2]

At the age of 64, Martin Rogers took on a challenge— learning how to read and write. But Martin had a specific goal. He wanted to read the 23rd Psalm by Christmas, which was only a few months away.

As a child, Martin had dropped out of school in the third grade. Shortly thereafter, he went to work in a textile plant. He subsequently married, raised seven children, and was active in his church. It saddened him that he was unable to read the Bible. As chairman of the deacons, he felt that all deacons should know how to read Scripture. He was determined to try.

Martin did realize his goal. On Christmas, he proudly read the 23rd Psalm in front of the whole congregation. It was something he never dreamed he'd be able to do before he set his goal.

"Before this, I wouldn't get up before the congregation," Martin said, "but I don't mind getting up now and doing the best that I can. I'm enjoying every hour and every minute of it." [3]

TENTMAKERS

I was reminded recently that many of us are "tentmakers;" in other words, we are in God's service but earning our own living. The apostle Paul was a tentmaker, working at his profession even as he served God. Scores of preachers and pastors, especially in smaller churches, are tentmakers, not taking a salary from the church but having an outside job to support themselves.

To these preachers, their "call from God" is a spiritual experience. God didn't wait for them to get an education. After the call, a considerable number are returning to education to help them fulfill their pledge of service.

Be doers of the word,
and not merely hearers...
Faith by itself,
if it has no works,
is dead.

James 1:22, 2:17
(New Revised Standard Version)

VOLUNTEERS WHO WANT
TO TEACH READING/WRITING

t was Maundy Thursday, just before Easter. As a Christian, I was attending my church service, taking communion. Included was the Tenebrae service.

The Tenebrae service is an expressive drama in which eight church elders read portions of the Bible, helping the communicants to re-live the days and experiences of the early Christians. A candle was set before each participant. The flame was snuffed out upon completion of the reading, leaving the sanctuary in complete darkness.

It was a moving experience, but as I listened I realized that if you couldn't read, you couldn't take a leading part in this service. Certainly being able to read shouldn't be a criterion. Yet, without this ability one cannot be a part of the ceremony. We take being able to read so for granted. Once we realize the importance of reading in our worship service, we are challenged to help others learn this basic skill.

εν αρχη ην ο λογος, και ο λογος ην
προς τον θεον, και θεος ην ο λογος.

These are words from the Bible, words that you know but are unable to read unless you read Greek. Perhaps in trying to read these words you'll understand a bit of the frustration a non-reader feels when trying desperately to read from his Bible. The words in English are from John 1:1 —

In the beginning was the Word, and the Word was with God, and the Word was God.

When you are considering tutoring with a focus on reading the Bible, look first to your own motivation. If your goal is to convert a person to your own beliefs, I'd suggest you look elsewhere. But if you want to open doors to others so they can read the Bible and search for themselves, if you're willing to show by example, then perhaps this book can be helpful. A positive way to share your beliefs is through your actions. Show love, patience, kindness—these actions speak louder than words.

In a one-to-one (OTO) or small group setting, we're looking to help adults who have *chosen* the Bible as their reading material in order to read better. It is not up to the tutor or the facilitator to interpret the Bible for the students, but rather to encourage these students to think, to question, and to explore for themselves.

Your goal is to help students not only read biblical passages they may already know, but to help them find new, unknown passages. Maybe some will learn how the Bible is set up so that they can refer to specific passages, master the words of church hymns, or discover biblical stories from other books. The students set personal goals and choose the material to be used in the tutoring sessions. As the facilitator, the tutor helps them attain these goals.

CAN I DO IT?

I don't pretend to be an authority on the Bible, but I *can* read it, and I know how to teach reading. I'm willing to focus the lessons on topics and materials my individual student or those in my group want. In this instance that means the Bible or other religious materials.

You may ask, "Can I help others to read the Bible when I'm not a student of the Bible myself or even a Sunday School teacher?" Or, "Will I be a good tutor, knowing biblical stories but having no background in teaching?"

The desire to help and the willingness to give time to teaching reading and writing are not enough. Even the desire to help someone know more about the Bible is not enough. Effective tutoring comes at least in part from learning the skills and techniques of teaching basic reading and writing, being sensitive to each student's needs and goals, and giving time to lesson planning as well as teaching.

Patience, enthusiasm, and a commitment to teaching are also

essential to good tutoring. Whatever your previous training, some of the skills you already have will help you to gain the "how to" skills you will need.

Be aware of the personal qualities that are important...

- Patience
- Empathy
- Understanding/Respect
- A Sense of Humor
- Creativity
- Adaptability
- Sensitivity
- Enthusiasm
- Realistic Expectations [4]

... and know that you, too, will be a learner. You'll probably learn new ways to help others, and you'll certainly learn more about your students as they share their experiences with you. You'll uncover worship practices different from your own. You may be invited to your students' places of worship. What a privilege to be able to teach, learn, and share!

Take my family, for example. Our son and his family are active in an Evangelical church in which they use tambourines, drums, and enthusiastic singing with hands raised along with voices. It is quite a contrast to our more serene Presbyterian church with organ music and a traditional liturgy, or our daughter's United Methodist church with its fervent singing and warm fellowship.

A Quaker meeting reminds me of the strength of quiet times and prayer, while the Catholic and Episcopal services recall the sacredness of Mass and Communion. Visiting all-black churches gives me the emotional and warm, deep-souled feelings reminiscent of my childhood in a Swedish Evangelical church. Attending Sabbath services at a local synagogue reminds me of Jesus, a devout Jew, worshipping in the temple in Jerusalem, learning from the rabbis.

We are entitled to our opinions and interpretations of the scriptures. We have this freedom because we have learned to read it for ourselves. As you work with people of other persuasions, remember the Judeo-Christian commitment of love, accepting people where and how they are. As reading tutors, it is not our job to teach theology.

Be *kind* to one another,
tenderhearted,
forgiving one another.

Ephesians 4:32
(New Revised Standard Version)

RECRUITING AND COMMITMENT

$\mathcal{H}$ow do you reach adults who want to learn specifically to read the Bible, to let them know that you would like to help them?

Much of the time, tutors are already working with adults in a literacy program, helping to improve their reading and writing. Together they search out and identify goals of the students, pinpointing reading the Bible as a primary goal. Having had previous training, tutors can use and adapt the suggestions given in this book.

In getting background information on potential students, literacy providers often find that some of these adults have already identified reading the Bible as their reason for wanting to improve their reading and writing skills. If they have a list of trained tutors who are interested in teaching these skills focusing on the Bible, the information in this book will provide the additional training they may need.

If you are thinking of starting a small group with Bible reading as the focus of the reading/writing efforts, you might ask your literacy program to get the word out to current students. Some might want to add a small group activity specifically relating to the Bible to their present one-to-one tutoring.

You may be a part of a church community in which you see the need for help in learning to read the Bible, or you have been asked for help by such a group. Getting training is essential—or at least reading and practicing techniques such as those suggested in *TUTOR.*[5] Then you can use and adapt the suggestions given here.

GETTING STARTED

If it is suggested that you recruit your own students, even within an organized literacy program, how do you start? A good first step would be talking to preachers and pastors in inner-city churches, as well as ministers of small rural and large city churches. Many communities have a Council of Churches or an Interreligious or Lay Leadership Council to which area churches and religious organizations belong. They probably could assist in identifying where there is a need. Once you have identified specific churches, tell the pastor or preacher your plans, and ask if you may talk to his deacons, deaconesses, or other members of the congregation.

Plan your talk well, limiting it to 10-15 minutes. You might want to bring various versions of the Bible — *The Good News Bible* or *The Bible for Students* with their simple print and colorful illustrations, as well as other basic Bible or religious stories.[6] Be careful not to bring material aimed at children. Let your audience know that prospective students will pick out the material to be used to help improve their reading and writing.

Assure your audience that you will *not* be interpreting the Bible or giving your views. You will be teaching them to *read for themselves*, so that they can form their own opinions. Assure them that you will be teaching them to *read*. They may already know as much or more about the Bible than you do.

Let them know some of your plans:

- Teaching reading and writing skills will be the basis of the lessons.
- The material used in teaching these skills will be Bible oriented and chosen by the students.
- The lessons will go at the pace of the students.
- The lessons can be one-to-one or within small groups of three to five.
- You will work on fluency in helping them to read the Bible publicly before their congregations.
- You will meet for one- or two-hour sessions each week at a place convenient to the students.

- The students need to make a commitment to attend regularly for at least three months and to set aside 15 minutes a day for at least five days a week for Bible or Bible-related reading
- You will *not* be interpreting the Bible or giving your views, but will be teaching reading so that the students can read and interpret for themselves
- You will act as a facilitor as you work together, helping the students attain *their* goals.
- You are a volunteer.

If the information is advertised in a church bulletin, it is vital that the class be listed as a "Reading Class Using the Bible" rather than a "Bible Study Class." This will avoid initial confusion.

A BEGINNING

Several years ago, I had a small group which focused on reading with children. This was a most successful project, culminating in the publication of *Reading With Children* by Lester Laminack, Ed.D., and a training video.[7]

Martha had been a member of this small group. Martha's reading improved greatly during our sessions, and she continued to improve with her own tutor. Yet she wanted more. She wanted to be able to read the Bible better, to understand the words, to be able to discuss and write about various passages.

Martha worked as community organizer for a Christian community center. She knew other women who had similar goals. She didn't know their reading levels, but recognized they needed help and wanted to focus their reading lessons on the Bible.

The Christian community center was the recipient of free surplus food, but Martha found that there were some items that the women weren't taking. They said they didn't like them. Martha knew the food was good and nourishing and that the women did not know how to prepare them so that they tasted good.

The two items in question were brussel sprouts and squash. So Martha had a luncheon, inviting women of the community. She invited me also. She included these two vegetables, tastefully cooked and attractively prepared. We all enjoyed the food.

The luncheon also provided an opportunity for us to get acquainted. I had a chance to explain my project—a small group to help with reading, focusing on the Bible. Some of these women became the nucleus of our small group.

Let me introduce you to the women in my first Bible reading small group. They're proud of their accomplishments and have given me permission to use their names and stories:

Dorothy, 34, is a single parent with four children, pregnant with a fifth. She has had little schooling and now has little self-confidence, evidence of low self-image, and is looking for friendship. Dorothy is lovely and determined to learn, but she was hospitalized for part of our sessions and, with her family responsibilities, came when she could. Her reading tested at a 2nd grade level.*

Leola, 41, is a mother of five, grandmother of two. She is extremely shy and lacks self confidence, yet is the "salt of the earth," a true friend to each of us. Leola resisted writing for she had never had help even with forming her letters. She's a dedicated church woman and grandmother. She had had four years of schooling; her reading tested at approximately the 2nd grade level.

Ruth, 39, is a mother of four, grandmother of eight, and a devout church member. She had 11 years of schooling but could read and comprehend at only a functional level. She said she doesn't remember what she reads. Ruth is very quiet, seldom talks, but while resisting writing at first, we've found that she can express herself well in writing.

* Students' reading levels were determined through LVA's *Reading Evaluation Adult Diagnosis (READ)* .[8]

Martha, 46, is a natural leader. She was born in the South, worked in the cotton fields even as a child, and had few opportunities to go to school. Martha and her husband have four children and have struggled to buy a house that they're fixing up. Martha is determined to get an education. She's brought her reading level to above 5th grade. Martha is truly the leader of our group.

I recruited my second small group for this study by talking to the pastor of a city church, explaining my program to help improve reading and writing by focusing on biblical materials. Because my first group consisted of all women, I hoped to have this group consist of only men. I asked if I could talk to his congregation. He agreed, and I carefully planned my 15-minute talk, using the Bible, posters of biblical stories, and samples of simply written books as I demonstrated how I planned to help them choose their own materials. My job, I explained, would be to teach them what they wanted, to act as facilitator to help them attain their own goals.

While my talk was greeted with enthusiasm and many "Amens," no one volunteered to attend. It was only later, as we chatted together, that three men discreetly came to me to find out more. I invited them to meet with me to explore together and see if this might be what they wanted.

Let me introduce these three men with whom I have worked as we shared our knowledge of biblical stories:

Freeman is in his 60s, a good talker, and an excellent crafts-man with wood and metal. Freeman only went to the first grade, could write only his name, not his address, and didn't know the names of all the letters of the alphabet. Freeman stayed in the group for several months, but eventually got his own tutor. He needed individual help.

Sam, too, is in his 60s. He went to the 7th grade and served in the army. He's married, has children, grandchildren, and a great-grandchild. He's active in his church and wants to be able to read the Bible from the pulpit. His reading level was about 4th grade.

James is a senior deacon, being responsible for all the maintenance and construction in the church. James went to the 10th grade and is such a personable, likable, capable man that I was surprised that his reading level was only 2nd grade. His comprehension is excellent and he's so dependable, doing every bit of homework required.

SIGNING ON THE DOTTED LINE

As I look back, I see I was idealistic—and there's nothing wrong with being idealistic—but in reality things did not quite work out the way I had planned. Even though all signed an agreement to read or write 15 minutes a day, they did not do so. It took months for them to *want* to do extra work at home. They didn't show up at every meeting or call me as they had promised. I found that a telephone call the night before a lesson usually ensured their prompt attendance.

I was pleased when they finally took their responsibilities seriously. It made me realize the importance of stressing the commitment of each student. This I had failed to emphasize at the beginning of our lessons together. There must be standards, and if those standards are not held, something must be done, perhaps even terminating the lessons. Having the group members make the ground rules—having *them* responsible for keeping the rules—helps strengthen student commitment. Peer pressure is a great help in enforcing the ground rules.

I had suggested six weeks as a trial period. I soon realized that this was too short a time, for it took that long just to get acquainted. We agreed that a three-month commitment should be a minimum for a start. At the end of each three-month period the group could decide if they wanted to continue for another three months. This proved to be a good way. It gave them and me an "out," yet also gave opportunities to continue easily.

All the members of both groups agreed to read or write at least 15 minutes a day for at least five days a week. I agreed to have materials and lesson plans ready. We agreed to call each other if, for any reason, we could not attend any session or be on time. Each of us, including me, signed a simple agreement, a sample of which appears in the appendix. Feel free to copy it or adapt it to the needs of your own student.

After the first three months, we talked about the possibility of having someone else join our group. The members of both groups felt they would prefer keeping it as it was. It had taken us that long to really "bond," to feel free to admit our needs and seek help from each other. Clearly the idea of bringing a "stranger" in at this stage was viewed as far too disruptive.

Even though my students did not adhere completely to the agreement that each had signed, they decided it was a good idea to have it. They said I should have explained it in more detail, letting them know that it was a real commitment, that I expected them to live up to it, that the consequences could be no more lessons.

Mutual agreement and trust are important in any learning situation, and it's helpful to discuss expectations beforehand.

I will instruct thee
and teach thee
in the way thou shalt go.

Psalms 32:8
(King James Version)

TECHNIQUES FOR
TEACHING READING/WRITING

*T*his book is written to help those tutors who want to teach basic reading and writing skills to adults who have specifically indicated they want to read the Bible. It suggests using the whole language approach which includes using all the language skills—listening, speaking, reading, and writing. If you are not familiar with ways to teach reading and writing using whole language, you may want to read *TUTOR*, LVA's handbook giving detailed, "how-to" instructions on the necessary techniques.[9] Language experience, sight words, phonics, patterned words, and process writing are included. However, all these techniques will be described in this book as they can be applied to teaching reading/writing focusing on biblical materials.

While I chose to work within a small group setting, I have worked one-to-one with many students. The techniques described are applicable to both.

Reading isolated words or even sentences without comprehension is not really reading. Understanding what is being read is most important. You must make sure that all lessons reflect comprehension.

Because each student has different needs, strengths, and weaknesses, you must be able to focus on individual problems. Using a whole language approach ensures that comprehension is the basis of all teaching, but specific techniques can be incorporated into the learning. In order to do this, you must be familiar with a variety of teaching techniques. All of these can be adapted to use within the content area your students have chosen—in this case, biblical material.

LANGUAGE EXPERIENCE

Using the learner's own experiences and words as the basis for reading material is an effective way of involving students right from the first lesson. It is an excellent "ice breaker" as well as a practical way of getting insight into the learner's world.

An experience story is an expression in the learner's own words. It could be a memorized verse of the Bible that he wants to read. It could be a church or Sunday School experience of his childhood, or a retelling of an Old Testament story or one of Jesus' parables. It can be an individual's story, or it can be a group story.

The tutor prints, in manuscript, the words dictated by the students, writing exactly as the students talk, not correcting grammar but spelling the words correctly. If it's a group story, write it on a blackboard or on a large pad, copying it later. You may also use a computer if one if available. If it's for an individual student, use carbon paper so that you can both have a copy.

Use manuscript writing because it's nearer the printed pages your students want to read. Cursive writing, connecting the letters, will come later. You may want to practice your own manuscript writing. There are samples of both in the appendix.

The tutor reads the story aloud, pointing to each word as read, then asks the students to read the story aloud. Each sentence may be reread several times if necessary.

Next, suggest that the students pick out meaningful words that they'd like to study. Underline these words in the story, and put each word on a small card. When this is a group story, use index cards, but when teaching one-to-one, quartered index cards are more convenient. Teach these special words out of context as whole words, matching the word cards with the words in the story.

Have the students return to the story, rereading it. They can copy the story from the blackboard, and also copy the meaningful words on cards. Or give individual students the original writing for home practice. You keep a copy for your records. This exercise can lead to the students writing their own stories.

When Leola and Freeman wrote their names and addresses on index cards at the first meeting, I saw that they had difficulty even printing individual letters. I noted that they were hesitant to read, even with the others in the small group. This alerted me that Leola and Freeman were beginning readers/writers. The language experience approach would be an excellent beginning for them.

At an early session, while the others were writing their stories (to be discussed later in "Process Writing"), Leola and I sat together, and quietly she told this story. I wrote the words as she dictated, teaching her her own words.

> I was born in Dillon, South Carolina. I had it hard. I picked cotton with family and friends. The only time I went to school was when it rained. I didn't have that much school.

> The most important thing in my life now is being happy. I love my church. I like my group.

This was the "ice breaker" for Leola. She was comfortable knowing that she didn't have to do all the things the others did. We had a good beginning.

Language Experience

1. Identify an experience by conversation.
2. Record the learners' words exactly as spoken.
3. Read the story; ask the students to read the story.
4. Together select meaningful words for instruction.
5. Put these target words on index cards, teaching them as whole words.
6. Have students match the words on the cards with those in the story.
7. Have students reread the story.
8. Give a copy of the story and words cards to students for home practice.
9. Progress from dictating to writing.

SIGHT WORDS/CONTEXT CLUES

Sight words are those words immediately recognized and understood by the reader. They are learned as whole units, and are an important part of any reading.

Beginning readers often know many words by sight from memory. These words often trigger the meaning of a complete sentence which includes new words. This ability to note what makes sense is called *using context clues* and is a skill we all use in our reading.

Many of the words taught in experience stories are taught as sight words—as whole words—but there are other words that must be taught similarly: survival words (*poison, emergency*), service words (*the, but, how*), irregularly spelled words (*of, where*), and introductory words in a patterned series (*old* when teaching *told, sold, cold*).

Here's a basic way to teach sight words:

Sight Words

1. Pick one word to be taught as a sight word.
2. Write that word in manuscript on an index card for a group, or a quartered index card for individuals.
3. Write that word in a sentence, underlining or highlighting the word.
4. Ask the students to look at the word and say the word aloud.
5. Ask the students to match the word card with the word in the sentence, saying the word aloud.
6. Put the card aside, and repeat steps 1 through 5 with another word.
7. When you have taught five words, shuffle the word cards and ask the students to read them. They can refer back to the sentences if they need help. Put a check (✔) on the back of each word card read correctly.
8. When a word has been read correctly at three separate lessons, it can be filed as "known" to be used later for reinforcement and practice.[10]

Personal sight word lists will come out of your students' experience stories and their writings. One of my students wrote "Prays the Lord." All the words were spelled and read correctly, but it gave me an opportunity to explain the difference between *praise* and *prays*. When another student wrote a description of Jesus stilling the turbulent waters, he wrote "Jesus cammd the ruff waters." He wanted all the words spelled correctly and asked for help, so *calm* and *rough* were included in his personal word list. As you include new words, be aware of how many more new words can be added in the same patterns: *rough* and *tough*, or *pray, say, stay, way,* and *sway.*

PHONICS

Phonics, the relationship of symbols or letters and sounds, is an important aspect of teaching reading. Because English is in large part phonetically irregular, its use is limited. However, it is important that tutors know how to teach letter/sound relationships. Detailed discussion and instruction are included in *TUTOR* and should be reviewed, but here is the "how-to" in a nutshell.

Because vowels do not have consistent sounds, only teach the individual sounds of consonants. Begin with those consonants with which students are having difficulty, or with those consonants important to an individual—perhaps those in his name or in words that are the most meaningful (i.e. *Bible, Messiah, God*). Consonant digraphs, in which two letters with one sound (*ch, sh, th, wh,* or *qu*), are taught in the same way, with words such as *church.*

Phonics

1. Identify the letter by giving its name, writing it in manuscript. ("This is the letter *m.*") *
2. Ask the student to listen to the beginning sound. ("Listen for the sound of *m* at the beginning of these words and repeat the words... *man, mission, mountain.*")

---

* (Note: *m* denotes the name of the letter; /*m*/ denotes the sound)[11]

3. Pick a key word. ("Which of these words, man, mission, mountain, do you want to help you remember the sound of *m*?"—Student picks *man*.)
4. Produce the beginning sound. ("Think of the beginning sound in *man*, and say the first sound."—/*m*/ is the sound of *m*.)
5. Recognize the sound in other words. ("Here are other words. Listen. Do they start with the *m* sound?—*Bible* [no], *messenger* [yes], *Sunday* [no], *majesty* [yes], *worship* [no].)
6. Put the sound at the end of words. ("I'll move the *m* sound to the end of words. Listen to the last sound and repeat the words—*rim, lumb* [no matter the spelling, the last *sound* is /*m*/], *Bethlehem*.")
7. Produce the ending sound. ("What is the last sound in these words?" /*m*/.)
8. Review. ("What is the name of this letter?" *m*. "Your key word?" *man*. "The sound?" /*m*/.)
9. Write the letter. ("Please write an *m*.")
10. Explain and write the capital letter. ("This is a capital *M*, the same name, the same sound. Write a capital *M*.")

VOWELS

Teaching the sounds of vowels can be a real challenge because a vowel can represent more than one sound. Frequently the sound the vowel represents can only be determined by noting the letters that follow it. Note the many ways *a* can sound in various patterns.

can

call

came

caw

car

Because English has many consistent patterns, it is more practical to teach vowels within word patterns.

WORD PATTERNS

The English language contains many patterns. Lists of patterns are in the Appendix of *TUTOR*. Seeing relationships between clusters of letters and the sounds they represent can help students read similar words. For instance, if a student can read *man*, and knows the sounds of the consonants *p* and *f*, he probably can easily read:

man

pan

fan

If he is taught *light* as a sight word, and he knows the sounds of the consonants *f* and *r*, he can probably read:

light

fight

right

Teaching words in pattern may seem simple, but it is well worth practicing because of its value.

It is helpful to *write* the words as they are spoken, putting them in a column so that similar letters in the pattern can be *seen* as well as heard. Here are the basic steps in teaching words in pattern:

Word Patterns

1. Write the first word in the pattern: man,
   followed by the second patterned word: pan.
2. Explain as follows: "If *m-a-n* is *man*, what is *p-a-n?*"
3. If the student responds correctly, add more words in pattern, asking the student to read them.

   ran
   can

   If the student gives no response or responds incorrectly, review elements of difficulty:

   a. He may not know the sound of the consonant.

   b. He may not know the sound of the letter cluster.

4. Ask the student to identify the letters of the words that are the same in all the words.
5. Make word cards for the words in pattern.[12]

PROCESS WRITING

Writing and speaking are forms of communication that *give information*, while reading and listening are forms that *receive information.*

WRITING (give information) SPEAKING

COMMUNICATION

READING (receive information) LISTENING

We are all communicating most of the time—sometimes very effectively, sometimes not so effectively. Let's zero in on writing as a form of communication.

Process Writing can be the logical step to follow dictation from experience stories. It can be used as a teaching technique on its own. It is a technique all of us use to solve our daily problems, whether it's writing lists to help us in shopping or writing letters of praise or complaint. It can also be used for informal assessment, showing the tutor where help is needed. Keeping on-going samples of students' writing can demonstrate progress made.

Here are the steps for process writing:

Process Writing
1. Present trigger event
2. Pre-Write
   a. Discuss
   b. Set the writing task
   c. Brainstorm
3. Write
4. Read/Respond
5. Revise/Rewrite
6. Edit/Rewrite[13]

Assure the students that spelling, grammar, and punctuation are not important at this time. You can work with those areas later. It is important at first just to get their words on paper. If a student cannot spell a word, suggest he write it as he thinks it should be, or write the first letter and a dash (i.e., *cherch* or *ch——* for *church*).

In our small group, we decided to concentrate on our own churches (1 - *Trigger event*), and we talked about what we liked best and when we were disappointed (2a - *Discuss*).

For their first writing project, the women decided they would like to try just writing how they felt (2b - *Set the writing task*). They zeroed in on specific things that happened to them within their church communities. Discussion brought out many ideas (2c - *Brainstorming*), and I encouraged them to write down *key words* to help them as they prepared for writing. If students are hesitant at first, you write key words as they talk. In our group, each came up with her own list of words and her own story.

Let me share two different stories (3 - *Write*). Read them, keeping in mind that you are looking for ways to help in future lessons and to come up with an informal assessment.

Dorothy's Key Words and Her Story

> ch _____
>
> Housekeeping
> talk of God
> my life

> I aten Bortherley Love Ch._____
> I the Rumber Kelep me with my
> Housekeeping on monday For About
> 1½hr and we talk About the god and Thing
> I want to Do with my life and Some of the thing
> is to be Albe to r_____

Dorothy's spelling and punctuation were far from perfect, but Dorothy knew what she wrote and read it aloud to us (4 - *Read*). The group liked what she had written, praising those church members for putting their Christian love into action. It is up to the tutor to encourage students to give comments and constructive criticism. (3 - *Respond*). Dorothy asked for help in spelling — she knew many of the words were not correct.

Do you remember the frustration of receiving a paper back in school, all marked up with corrections? It was so discouraging. But Dorothy did ask for help in spelling. You may also receive this request. Why not merely underline each word that is incorrectly spelled, put a number above it, and spell the word correctly with a corresponding number on another sheet of paper? For Dorothy, the process gave her the opportunity to revise and rewrite if she wanted to do that (5 - *Revise/Rewrite*). She elected not to edit and rewrite (6 - *Edit/Rewrite*).

Assessment—From Dorothy's writing I could assess where her strengths were and where she needed help. Dorothy had good ideas, could express herself well, but she needed help in spelling and in punctuation. She used uppercase and lowercase letters haphazardly. She formed her letters well, but Dorothy's writing alerted me that she probably was a beginning reader and writer.

Martha's Key Words and Her Story

Choir CONN   my members
joy to sing   it hurt
4 - 5 Hour ride

A few day ago My Church had a Choir
Come from CONN. To Sing, ⊙ What a joy
that was they Sing Oflt of their Heart
My Church Choir Sing also. These people
ride for 4 - 5 Hour to get here to put on
this program. My members did Not full Come
Out that hurt but they are faith members
If you ben born again in Christ you is New

Martha read her story (4 - *Read/Respond*), and everyone agreed with Martha that it was inconsiderate of the members not to show up. Martha not only asked for help in spelling, but realized some of the words were not written as she read them. She wanted to revise and rewrite (5 - *Revise/Rewrite*), and edit and rewrite (6 - *Edit/Rewrite*).

Assessment—Martha is a more advanced reader/writer, needing help in spelling, punctuation, and capitalization.

After they had rewritten their stories, I offered to type them. The typed copies of their letters were real inspirations to them. Somehow, anything that is actually in print seemed "more right" to them. And, to tell the truth, their simple writings did look very professional in type.

MECHANICS NEEDED IN WRITING

Handwriting—Because manuscript writing is nearer the type on printed pages, it is suggested that students learn to write in manuscript (print) first, followed by cursive (connecting the letters). However, if your students already write in cursive and prefer to write connecting the letters, adhere to the students' wishes. Both manuscript and cursive writing are needed skills. Samples of both manuscripts and cursive writing are in the appendix.

Punctuation and Capitalization—You can make your own drill sheets by using pages from any book your students are interested in. Rewrite the stories, putting the entire text in lowercase letters and omitting the punctuation. After explaining when to use capital letters and when to use periods or question marks, have the students correct the rewritten pages. In the appendix is a sample exercise sheet to help students understand when to use capital letters, periods, commas, and quotation marks.

God has given each of us
the ability to do
certain things well.
If you are a teacher,
do a good job of teaching.

Romans 12:6-7
(Bible for Students)

THE FIRST MEETING

*A*fter you have made your commitment to teach, have had training or read a basic reading manual such as *TUTOR*, have read through this book, and have been assigned or recruited your students, you will want to plan for your first meeting together.

It is not unusual for tutors, both new and veterans, to be a bit nervous, get "butterflies in their stomachs." If you are nervous because this is a new experience for you or because you do not know how your students will react, think how adult students feel. They have had so many failures that they, too, may be hesitant. Do they want to expose themselves to another failure? Will this new teacher really help and encourage them?

With these thoughts in mind, be sensitive to the feelings of the students, especially during that first hour together. A positive session will bring them back. So, it is up to *you* to plan well and to bring the appropriate materials.

WHAT TO BRING TO A LESSON

It is helpful to keep your materials together in a bag, a briefcase, or a large folder. You might want to include the following, although you will certainly add other materials you find helpful as you go along:

- *In the Beginning Was the Word: Teaching Reading and Writing Through the Bible*
- *TUTOR*
- Folder for your records on students
- Background information on each student
- Name tags
- Folder, paper, pen for each student
- Testing material for evaluation
- Copies of Agreement, Study Time Sheets (see appendix)
- Bible stories, simply written (see bibliography)

- Posters or pictures of biblical stories for discussion
- Hymn book or copies of special hymns
- Index cards for class use, quartered index cards for individual student use
- Extra paper, carbon paper
- Inspirational stories to be read
- Lesson plans for the meeting
- Bible for each student

Some churches make the *King James Version* (KJV) of the Bible their only option. If so, ask if the pastor will accept the *New King James Version* which changes "thees" and "thous" to normal English but keeps true to the KJV translation. You might suggest the *Good News* version or the *Bible for Students* as a good way to learn to read the Bible, with the assurance that students can read other versions later. Tell them to refer to the KJV for pulpit usage.

If you have limited funds, you might obtain matching Bibles for yourself and your students by asking around at various churches to see if they have used or extra Bibles. It is often surprising the stacks of slightly used Bibles of various versions that you may find in church storerooms. While it is helpful for the students and tutor when reading together, it is also interesting to compare the same verses in other Bibles, encouraging discussion and questions.

There are many versions of the Bible. The bibliography in the Appendix lists several. Do not choose a Bible until you have looked over several versions. Continue looking and asking until you find what you want. If you make your wants known, perhaps in church bulletins, parishioners often will be glad to give funds to purchase whatever versions of the Bible you want. The American Bible Society provides Bibles at greatly subsidized prices. And you might get used hymnals from your own or other churches, too.

I believe we are stewards of our funds and our materials. If I can save by getting materials donated, I can use whatever funds I do get for other needed books or material.

TIME, PLACE, AND EQUIPMENT

You have set up a meeting place and time for your first meeting. After you have met together, discuss if this place and time are suitable for future meetings:

- Is there enough security? (A church or a library is usually in a lighted and secure area)
- Is the light bright enough?
- Are the tables and chairs adequate?
- Is the temperature satisfactory?
- Is there a blackboard or place to write, especially if you have a small group?
- Is it too noisy?
- Do you have enough privacy?
- Are you and your students comfortable working here?

INTRODUCTIONS

In the center of the table around which you will be sitting, set up a display of some of the materials you suggest using with your students. Looking through the material gives newcomers an opportunity to adjust to this new situation. When working with one person, you can sit next to one another or across from each other—whichever is most comfortable. A round table is preferable for a small group, for then there is no "head" of the table. But most tables are oblong. Vary the seating so that different people sit at the head of the table. The tutor can easily sit at the side of the table with an easel or chalkboard behind her.

That first meeting together, whether it is you and one student or you and a small group, is so important. You are setting the climate for future get-togethers. I suggest that you have name tags for each, yourself included, with each name *largely* written in manuscript (printing).

Seeing as well as saying a name helps stamp it in our minds. Name tags save the embarrassment of forgetting names, especially for a small group with participants who do not know each other. I usually put both the first and last name on the name tag.

When you are meeting with one student, it is easy to introduce yourself and greet your student by name. When meeting with a small group, you may want to model a simple introduction. You may have some background information on the students (age, marital status, children, education, job, the churches attended), but they know little about you. That's why I find it helpful to share with them some information about myself—my husband's name, the number of children and grandchildren we have, where I was born, something about a hobby or what I like to do, and the church I attend.

Invite the participants to talk a little about themselves. Having seen your introduction, they know what to expect and thus are better able to relax as they introduce themselves.

LEARNING TOGETHER

Discuss together the purpose and goals of the meetings. Let them know that reading and writing better will be built into all lessons. Assure them that *they* will decide the materials to be used as well as the ground rules. You will be responsible for providing materials, but you should also encourage them to bring in reading matter that they want help with, too.

Together talk about commitment and responsibility. As tutor and facilitator, you have certain responsibilities. Your responsibilities are to:

- Be present and prepared for each meeting.
- Search out and bring material needed to fulfill the goals set forth.
- Plan ahead, always keeping in mind the wishes of the students.
- Let the students know well in advance if you cannot be present at any meeting.

- Make informal evaluations of individuals and/or the small group, sharing such information with the students.
- Keep a folder or portfolio with samples of student writings together wtih other pertinent information.

As students and learners, each one must also take responsibilities, recognizing that the absence of even one member affects the entire group. Each learner should agree to:

- Be present at each meeting.
- Be prepared to participate.
- Be on the alert for materials he wishes included in the sessions.
- Do a minimum of 15 minutes home practice every day.
- Call the tutor or facilitator well in advance if he cannot attend any meeting.
- Be willing to help with evaluations of the meetings by talking about what he found helpful or not helpful and what he liked best.
- Keep a folder or his written work, bringing it to each session.

Discuss the above responsibilities and commitments (the "ground rules") together. After agreeing or disagreeing and adding new items, suggest that all sign an agreement, affirming the group's wishes. Discuss again the agreed-upon times and place. Emphasize the importance of serious commitment to this agreement. You or the students not adhering to the agreement could cause the lessons to end.

Give each student a folder, suggesting that all written material be kept in this portfolio. Suggest that each one write his name and address on the outside with the time, date, and place for each meeting. Make sure to give your students your telephone number so that they can call you in an emergency.

Ask each one to write his or her name, address, and telephone number on an index card or paper for you. Let your students know that you, too, will keep separate folders for all your students, noting their work and progress.

You might want to share with your students a suggested format for the sessions. Knowing how you plan to conduct the

lessons eases tensions and gives them a framework to keep in mind.

If you are working with one student, you probably are meeting for an hour, twice a week. But if you are meeting with a small group, you might have two-hour sessions at least once a week. Know that within each group, each lesson or portion of a lesson can be expanded or adjusted, but it's helpful for students to know you have a general plan. Suggested lesson formats are included in Chapter 7.

You are encouraged to give the learners a paperback Bible, telling them that they may want to bring their own Bible from home too, but that you think it is helpful to have a study Bible in which they can write notes. These Bibles are theirs; suggest that they write their names inside the front cover. This gives you an opportunity to open the discussion of what the Bible is.

I had given each student a copy of *Good News for Modern Man*, saying, "This is the Bible." But I suddenly realized that this was *not* the whole Bible, only the New Testament, the Christian Scriptures. It gave me the opportunity to explain that the Bible is divided into two parts—the Old and the New Testament.*

Silence!

Did this mean that they didn't know there were two parts, or that they didn't know me well enough to say, "Of course, we know that." I asked, "Do you know the difference between the Old and the New Testament?"

Again, silence.

Didn't they know or were they too shy or too unfamiliar with me to answer?

Clearly they were not about to tell me, so I decided to plunge ahead and explain as simply as I could. "The Old

*The term "Old Testament" is the vernacular Christian term for the Hebrew Scriptures. While over 2,500 years old, the term "old" does not mean outdated. The word *testament* means *covenant*. The use of the term *Old Testament* in this story reflects the wording as it occurred in the class.

Testament is the early history of the Jewish people, and a basic guide to all facets of their lives. The New Testament is the story of Jesus and his disciples and followers."

I wrote *Old Testament* and *New Testament* on the board. The students read it, knowing what those words meant. Comprehension is basic to all teaching.

As I wrote *Old Testament,* I realized I could check to see how well they understood patterned words. I asked them to read the words as I wrote:

Old	*Testament*
cold	*best*
told	*rest*
sold	*nest*

The students had no problem with the words in these two columns, but when I added *fold,* two in the group faltered. I keep a separate sheet of paper with the heading "Error Chart," on which I make quick notes to remind me of where my students need help. Instead of interrupting the flow of a lesson to correct an error, I find it helpful to jot down and note where help is needed, giving me an opportunity to fit it into a later session.

The first notes on my Error Chart were reminders to teach the sound of the letter *f* to Leola and Freeman.

Depending on your students and the time left, you might want to get into teaching right off. You could ask the students what verses in the Bible they would like to work with first. With their suggestions given, you can go right into a lesson.

My group decided they wanted to read and write the 23rd Psalm. Already I was in trouble, for I had given them only the New Testament. But one must be adaptable, and I realized that this was an opportunity for a group "language experience" effort. I suggested they repeat the 23rd Psalm and I'd write it down.

"The Lord is my shepherd, I shall not want."

No problem. But there were differences of opinion for the next line. One said, "He maketh me to lie down." Another said, "He makes me lie down."

In our discussion, the group decided that both were right but that they would like me to write the second version. In the same way we continued to the end of the Psalm. We read it together, and they copied it from the board. I made word cards of special words they wanted—*Lord, shepherd, restored, soul*—and taught them those words as sight words. Many of the teaching techniques suggested in Chapter 4 were used even in that first lesson, according to the students' wants and needs.

They decided they wanted to rewrite the 23rd Psalm for homework and practice reading and writing the words on their special list. They asked me to type their final version of the 23rd Psalm. Both their handwritten copies and the typed copy were included in my and their portfolios.

Also have available an inspirational story to read aloud to the students near the end of each lesson. It can give the students a chance to relax and know that reading can be fun and stimulating as well. That first session sets the tone for the following lessons. Be sure to end the lesson on time, reminding them of the time and place for the next lesson.

HOME PRACTICE

Together you have decided how much time each student will give to home practice—at least 15 minutes a day. You can suggest that they rewrite some written material, read specific passages, review their own spelling or reading words, or whatever they are working on. I find that you must make it as easy as possible for adults to do home practice, because other work or family responsibilities often get in the way. Also, if you write down the suggested homework assignment, they are more likely to do it.

Just as the students have home assignments, so does the tutor. I find it easier to write up notes on what happened immediately after each session. It usually takes 15-20 minutes, but everything is fresh in my mind. From these notes, the next session's lesson plans come more easily.

If you have a copying machine available, make copies of each student's writing, giving a copy to the students and keeping the original for your portfolio. Often I mail these to my students. They like receiving mail, and it reminds them to do home practice.

Now is the time to put the written material from each student into their individual portfolios. Be sure to have each student write his name and the date on each paper—they can sometimes get mixed up.

Pick up your files, your materials, your lesson plans, knowing that you are already prepared for the next session—a nice feeling indeed.

Support each other
and build each other up.

I Thessalonians 5:11
(Bible for Students)

RESOURCES AND ACTIVITIES
FOR LESSONS

PASSAGES IN THE BIBLE

Many people who know passages from the Bible well do not know how to look up given passages. Your students may be able to quote John 3:16 and actually state that it is John 3:16, but not know how to find it in the Bible.

Show your students the list of books in the Old and New Testaments in the Table of Contents of the Bible, giving the page numbers. You may want to explain some of the abbreviations.

A first assignment could be giving names of various books to different students and having them actually find those books in their own Bibles. (Some students may already know how to do this and should have the opportunity to share this skill.) Then have them look up specific verses. Explain that the first number is the chapter, while the second number or numbers are the verses. Write several books, chapters, and verses on the board and ask the students to look them up.

John 3:16	Genesis 20:11-14
James 1:22	Esther 4:3-4
Ephesians 4:32	Job 19:25
Galatians 6:12	Psalms 55:22
Revelation 3:8	Isaiah 42:16

Depending on the reading levels of the students, you could suggest they read the verses either silently or aloud to the group. Discussion could center around slightly different wordings in various Bibles. The important thing here is that they know how to find passages in the Bible. Your students may have favorite verses which they have memorized or have framed on their walls. Now they can look at the references given at the end of these passages, find them in their Bibles, and read them for themselves.

Having a different biblical passage printed on the board or on paper for each lesson might be a good way to open a teaching session. Favorite verses stimulate discussion and questions. Encourage your students to bring in Bible verses to share, too.

WORDS OF HYMNS

When did you first learn that in reading the words to a hymn, you do not read line 1, then line 2, and 3, as you do in other reading? It may have come as a surprise to you as you tried to follow along, finally catching on that the words written to music are read and sung differently.

AMAZING GRACE

1. A - maz-ing grace-how sweet the sound-That saved a wretch like me!
2. 'Twas grace that taught my heart to fear, And grace my fears re - lieved;
3. Thru many-y dan - gers, toils and snares I have al - read - y come;

I once was lost but now am found, Was blind but now I see.
How pre - cious did that grace ap - pear The hour I first be - lieved!
'Tis grace hath brought me safe thus far, And grace will lead me home.

You read line 1 of each word grouping first, for that is the first verse, followed by the chorus if there is one. Then you return to the top of the page and read/sing line 2 of each word grouping, and the chorus. For the third verse you again return to the third line of that first section. As you go through a hymnal looking for favorite hymns, explain how you read/sing the verses. Your students may know this, but they may not. This might also be the time to explain contractions — 'Tis for *it is*, etc.

Singing is a popular part of any worship service. Some of us have sung many of the old hymns for years. We know the tunes; we know the words. Seeing those words in print and being able to read them would be a meaningful goal to many churchgoers. Find out the favorite hymns of your students, ask them to sing or say the words, and either you or they write them.

This could be the basis for an interesting and fun lesson. You will find many of the words repeated again and again, giving reinforcement to these words. Many of the words in popular hymns are an excellent base for teaching new words in pattern. Consider the following old favorite:

Count your many blessings, name them one by one.
Count your many blessings, see what God has done.
Count your many blessings, name them one by one.
Count your many blessings, see what God has done.

Ask your students if they can think of other words that rhyme with *count*. As they name the words, have them write the words and put them in a sentence. Go on to other words, e.g. *bless*, or *name*.

count	bless	name
mount	mess	same
fount	confess	tame

Your students may sing in their church choirs. They may have music with words they would like to learn to read. Suggest they bring their church music and together you can read it, using all the techniques you have learned. You could suggest they bring a tape recorder to choir rehearsal, tape the hymns sung, and together you can write, then read, the words.

Similarly, you can bring tapes of inspiring hymns or songs— *How Great Thou Art, The Hallelujah Chorus.* It may or may not be the first time your students have heard them. If you have words carefully printed or typed, you can easily use them as a reading lesson. And you might want to have the students read or sing the words with the tape. You may want to talk about the hymn, its history, its composer, who wrote the words, etc. Do you know the story of how *Amazing Grace* was written? John Newton wrote the words in the 1700s after his experiences as a heartless scoundrel and a slave trader who had a real change of heart.

From these readings, you can assess where your students need help. Were there any words they could not read? In reviewing these words, decide how you want to teach them— by sight, by having them guess using context clues, or perhaps by teaching in pattern. Again, this activity could set the stage for writing, using the song and its story as the trigger event around which you have discussion.

As one tutor and her student were working together, they realized they shared a love of music, especially hymns. They often ended their sessions together reading and softly singing favorite hymns.

BIBLICAL PICTURES/POSTERS

Many posters and pictures depict well-known Old and New Testament Bible stories or parables. Try to get a variety of artists' versions, letting your students pick the ones they want. You can get them from your own church or from religious book stores, and you might even want to include those depicting the same scenes with people of different races or ethnic backgrounds.

Christmas and Easter cards are excellent sources for different Christian biblical pictures. Pictures depicting Jewish or other religious stories can be found at synagogues or other places of worship. Save selected cards and keep a stack handy, using them to help interpret biblical events, showing how artists envision the same event differently.

While working in Mozambique, Africa, I found a fascinating set of biblical posters and cards where Jesus is depicted as a black African, and the settings are in rural Africa (see Bibliography). My African-American students, aware of and interested in their African heritage, often picked these as the "trigger event" as they began creating their own texts.

After these students had picked the picture they wanted to work from, and after discussion of the story or parable depicted, we read together that same story in a simplified form (See Bibliography for suggested Bible story series) and directly from their Bible. Then I suggested that they tell the story in their own words. Telling the stories can be done individually or as a group. Get group consensus on what is to be dictated.

At this point, I sometimes continue with the language experience technique (see Chapter 4). You might, however, suggest that students write their own version, becoming authors similar to other biblical authors. When students do their own writings, I sometimes intervene in the brainstorming session and often write key words on the blackboard as they identify them. Eventually they should write their own key words. Students use these words in preparation for writing their own stories.

James wrote these key words.

Jesus	
lota-poPle	Pheh
Fonner	Seed is The word of God
Stony	devil - Take
Plote-seeds	Stone-ShorT Time
Good Sold	weeds-Sin
Fell on	
Some-past-weed-binds	Dinds-
Jesus explaind	Good Soll examples

And here is James' story of the sower of seeds.

A Story of The Seed Sower

PeoPle kept comming To Jesus from Town
and village far and near large Chowd gathered
Jesus Told This parable.
Once a sower went out To sow Seed. As he
Scattered Seed in field. Some fell on The PaTh
They when Walk on. And The birds are Then;
Some of Then on rock, And when TheysPhouTed
They dried. Because The soil had no moisTune.
Some of The Seed-fell in The bushes, and They
were chocked. And some seed fell in good
ghound. And They sPhouTed uP. and bare one
hundredfold. And his discPles asked him.
whaT is This Pahble. Jesus said unTo Them
I given you Knowledge of The Kingdom
of God). BuT Some See it will noT undehsTand
Some will hear. BuT will noT undersTand.

Jesus ExPlains The STory of The Sower.
The Seed is The word of God. The seeds ThaT
fell on PaTh STand for Thoes who hear. BuT
leT SaTon Take iT away. The seeds ThaT
fell on rocky STand for Thos who hear
Wohd and receive iT WiTh Joy. BuT They

50

are over taking by temptation.
The Seeds that fell among thorn bushes
Stand for those who heare: But they
worries about thing of the world: And
theab fruit dies.
The seed that fell on good ground mean that
they hean the a word and obey it. And
keep. it. And all of theab pipens.

In my small groups, each student reads his own story. It is the same story, but each tells it a little differently. We continue through the steps of revising and rewriting.

BIBLE STORIES AND PARABLES

If your learners are better readers than writers or are reluctant to write, you may want to encourage them with some simple forms of help.

Select one simply written biblical story, with colorful illustrations, perhaps from Series A or B of the *American Bible Story* series or the *Bible for Students* (see Bibliography). If you are not sure of the reading level of any material you pick out, you can get an approximate grade level by using the Fry Readability Chart in the appendix.

Together, look at the pictures and discuss what the students *think* the story is about. They may or may not know the story. Together, you and your students read the story aloud.

Discuss the story, encouraging participation by asking questions. It is important to ask questions that will require more than a "yes" or "no" answer. (i.e. "Did you like the story?") Open ended questions are questions that require a more thoughtful answer.

- "Where did the story take place?"
- "Who were the important characters? Why? What did they do?"
- "Tell us more. Did you like this story? Why or why not?"

Have the students look up the same story in their Bibles—the text of any Bible story is usually noted at its end. If you have not previously shown them how to look up Bible passages, this is a good time to demonstrate that the numbers following the name of the book of the Bible indicate the chapters and verses.

Read together, silently and/or aloud, the passage from the Bible, followed by more discussion and questions.

- "Did you notice any difference in the two versions of the same story?"
- "Why do you think one had more details?"

Ask your student, or ask for a volunteer or a more advanced student from your group, to jot down key words as together you retell the story. Assure the writer that you and the other students will help with spelling and putting the ideas given into a single word or phrase. They may interrupt to remind the speaker of something that "came first." That shows that they are thinking and practicing sequencing skills.

With the outline of key words available, ask the students to write their own versions of the story. Remind them that spelling is unimportant at this time; if they're unsure of certain words they should write as best they can, putting down the first letter and a dash or spelling as much of the word as possible (i.e. *fathr* or *f——* for *father, heven* or *h —* for *heaven*).

Have the students read their own versions of the story. It is wise to encourage the lowest-level reader to go first, even if reluctantly, for it is more difficult for him if he has to follow someone who reads and writes at a higher level. Give praise and point out at least one positive attribute for each story.

Continue with the revising and rewriting until all students are satisfied with their own pieces.

STEPS FOR REWRITING A BIBLICAL STORY

(Tutor [T] and students [S] interact in this exercise.)

T&S   1. Select a biblical story, having a simplified version available, with illustrations, and noting where it is in the Bible.

T&S   2. Look at the pictures together and discuss them.

T&S   3. Read together the simplified story and discuss it.

S   4. Look up the same story in Bible.

T&S   5. Read together or individually the Bible version and discuss it.

S   6. Retell the story, writing key words.

S   7. Write individual versions of the story, using key words as an outline.

S   8. Read the story, getting feedback.

S   9. Revise, rewrite.

I type each student's story, giving each a copy and keeping a copy for individual portfolios. They like to see their own words in print as well as in their own handwriting. If you have a computer available, students can type in their own stories.

Once learners actually experience the stages—reading the story, participating in the discussion, writing the list of key words, writing the first and edited drafts of their stories, and finally seeing the typed story—motivation soars, and they are usually ready for more writing.

READING IN PUBLIC

Your students probably dream of reading aloud from the Bible from the pulpit in their churches, synagogues, or places of worship. They want to read fluently, not hesitantly, not word by word.

You can help them achieve this goal by working on phrase reading. Take any passage they want to read, and type it or write it carefully in manuscript. Leave enough space between lines for reading easily and for making slash marks.

After each student has read the passage silently, ask each one to read it aloud. Then, suggest that he look again at the material, thinking about words that seem to go together. Keep words in groupings such as phrases (although you need not talk of phrases), words that make sense together, or places where you take a natural breath.

Demonstrate how you would do this, and then make slash marks (/ /) between these natural word groupings. Suggest that your students make slash marks in the passage they read aloud. They might want to read groups of words silently before they write the slash marks.

There is no right or wrong place for the slash marks—in fact, those in the group might disagree as to where certain marks should be:

Blessed are / the poor in spirit, /
for theirs is / the kingdom of heaven. /
Blessed are / those who mourn, /
for they / will be comforted. /
or
Blessed are the poor in spirit, /
for theirs is the kingdom of heaven. /
Blessed are those who mourn, /
for they will be comforted. /   Matthew 5:3-4 (NRSV)

Suggest that your students read the passage again, this time reading silently the words between the slash marks before doing so aloud. They will notice, as you will, how much more meaningful the passage sounds. With practice, paying attention to slash marks, your students will read more fluently and more confidently.

READING THE BIBLE

Many students share the goal of reading an entire book in the Bible from beginning to the end. In fact, many want to eventually read the entire Bible. You might want to suggest that they start with the Gospel of Mark—it seems the simplest to read and several simplified versions of Mark are available (see Bibliography). Be sure you and your students have the same version of the Bible as you work together.

You may want to do a bit of research yourself, finding out something about Mark. You could then give a little historical background, telling how Mark learned of Jesus, how he went on missionary trips, and why he decided to write it all down.

As with any reading, you might want to suggest the students read the first eight verses in Mark silently before reading them aloud. Then, discuss the passage. You might want to compare this text in various versions of the Bible. You will probably come up with a personal word list for each student, words that they want help in reading. Knowing the various teaching techniques, you can now decide whether to teach these by sight or by pattern. You will discover which letter/sound combinations are problems for your students.

Use direct Bible reading as only one part of your teaching session. Vary your lessons to keep motivation high.

SYMBOLS

Our Judeo-Christian heritage is rich with symbols. Some are easily recognized while others are less known:

The *crucifix*, used within the Roman Catholic tradition, represents the suffering of Christ on the cross.

The *Latin cross*, used within most Protestant denominations, symbolizes the risen Christ, a sign of hope.

Other crosses used within Christendom: The *Maltese cross* - one of the "Crusader" crosses.

The *Tau cross* - shaped like the English letter *T*, a sign of immortality.

St. Andrew's cross - shaped like the letter *X*, on which Andrew, one of Christ's disciples, died.

Celtic cross - combination of the Latin cross and a circle, symbolizing eternity.

 The *fish* was a secret sign used by the early persecuted Christians to designate themselves as believers in Jesus.

 The *dove* expresses innocence and purity, signifying the Holy Spirit and the presence of God as hovering over the water at creation, and above Jesus at His baptism.

 A *dove with an olive sprig* sometimes is used as a symbol for the end of the great flood, denoting peace, forgiveness, and anticipation of new life.

 Candles are used throughout Christian worship services, signifying that light pushes away darkness and that Jesus is the light of the world.

 The *Star of David* is a six-pointed star sometimes shown as two interlocking triangles. It often identifies a Jewish building, persons, or grave.

 The *Star of Bethlehem*, a four-pointed star in the dimension of the cross, is symbolic of the birth of Jesus.

 The *Christmas Star*, a five-pointed star, representing Epiphany. It symbolizes the visit of the Magi to the infant Jesus and is celebrated on January 6th.

Your students might look around their places of worship and in their religious literature for other symbols. Researching and reading about their meanings can help make fascinating lessons.

PRAYER

What is prayer? One definition is that it is communication with God. But we must remind ourselves that communication is a two-way street, *listening* as well as *talking*.

Your students may have favorite prayers, perhaps some of the Psalms or the Prayer of St. Francis of Assisi. They may have memorized parts, have them framed at home, but would like to read them. You may have some favorite prayers to share with them, too.

My students wanted to read the Lord's Prayer, but directly from the Bible. As often as you have prayed the Lord's Prayer, I would guess that many of you, like me, are not exactly sure where it is in the Bible.

It is found in both Matthew (6:9-13) and Luke (11:2-4). You will probably find that neither one records it exactly as you say it, and much depends on the translation you use. And there is always the differences of using *debtors*, or *those who trespass against us*. With whatever your students feel most comfortable, whichever words are more meaningful to them, that is the way they will want to see it in print and how you should suggest your students write it.

Even before we looked it up in the Bible, I had my students write the words of the Lord's Prayer as *they* said it. We each had slightly different wording, but we agreed that all our versions meant the same thing.

MAPS

Most Bibles contain at least one map. Some show the Near East in ancient times, with Palestine and Jerusalem of the Hebrew Scriptures as well as of the New Testament. Others show Paul's journeys or the Roman Empire. Your students can locate places they have heard about on the map, learning to read and understand better how history really happened.

RELIGIOUS HOLIDAYS

Christians celebrate many holidays, but some are more widely known than others. Reading material describing them is abundant. Some holidays you may wish to utilize are discussed below.

Advent is the four weeks before Christmas during which Christians prepare to celebrate the birth of Jesus.

Christmas celebrates the nativity, the birthday of Jesus Christ.

Lent symbolizes Jesus' 40 days in the wilderness and is currently used as a preparation for the celebration of Easter.

Ash Wednesday is the first day of Lent, during which Christians request forgiveness, intending not to sin again. On Ash Wednesday, ashes are sometimes placed symbolically on the forehead at special church services.

Palm Sunday celebrates Jesus' triumphal entry into Jerusalem and begins Holy Week.

Holy Week is the week between Palm Sunday and Easter Sunday, which includes Maundy Thursday and Good Friday.

Maundy Thursday or *Holy Thursday* commemorates the institution of the sacrament of the Lord's Supper prior to Jesus' trial and execution.

Good Friday commemorates and mourns the death of Jesus Christ on the cross.

Easter celebrates the resurrection of Jesus Christ.

Pentecost celebrates the outpouring of the Holy Spirit and the birth date of the Christian church.

Don't overlook the Jewish holidays. Your students will be learning to read new Hebrew words as they learn more of history and their heritage.

Shabbat, the *Sabbath*, is the day of rest which marks the seventh day of the creation, when God rested from His labors. Jews remember and observe it with a day of rest, relaxation, study, and worship. It is traditionally celebrated from sundown Friday to sundown Saturday.

Rosh Hashanah means head of the year, when Jews observe the New Year and begin the 10 days of repentance. During that period, Jews are supposed to reflect on the past, atone to God with prayer for errors, and to apologize to wronged humans.

Yom Kippur is the day of atonement, when Jews believe they are judged by God for the coming year. This holiest day of the Jewish calendar year ends the 10 days of repentance. On it, Jews observe a complete 24-hour fast and, as a community, pray to atone for their errors.

Passover or *Pesach* recalls the Exodus from Egypt. Jews symbolically relive going from slavery to freedom with the special holiday ritual and meal, the *Seder*, and by eating matzot, unleavened bread, for seven days.

Succot, the feast of booths, originally celebrated the harvest, but now recalls the Israelite's 40 years of travels through the wilderness with Moses after the Exodus from Egypt.

Purim joyously celebrates the Book of Esther. Jews recall Mordecai's and Esther's victory the first time a villain, Haman, tried to annihilate them.

Shavuot celebrates Moses receiving the Ten Commandments and the Torah.

Hanukkah is not mentioned in the Bible, but is celebrated by many Jews as the festival of lights, celebrating Judah the Maccabee's victory over the Greco-Syrians.

DICTIONARY SKILLS

Most adults know the alphabet, the order of the letters, but many need practice in alphabetizing skills. Some people do not realize that alphabetizing goes to the second and third letters in words or names as well as the first letter. You can make your own list of words or names for practice, or you can use the sample sheets in the appendix.

Practice is often needed in looking up the meaning of words in the dictionary. Work together to make a list of words that need clarifying for your students. Looking these words up in a dictionary can give the stimulus for good discussion as well as practice in using the dictionary. A project could be to have your students write these definitions down and make their own Bible dictionary. An easy-reading Bible dictionary is suggested in the bibliography.

It is impossible for you to answer all the questions that could be put to you concerning the Bible. It is not up to you to answer your students' biblical questions. But you can help them answer their own questions. Emphasize your role as a reading teacher.

If you are asked, "What is baptism?" you could respond by asking, "How do they baptize in your church?" If a student asks how it is done in your church, you could respond by explaining that baptism is done differently in various churches, and tell them how it is done in your church. Do not let it seem that you are saying that yours is the only right way. You can always suggest that the students look the word up in the dictionary.

LITANIES AND BULLETINS

An excellent way to practice reading aloud is to include various litanies in your lessons. In most, there are alternate parts for the leader and the congregation to read. Get samples of these from various religious documents, and take turns being the leader or the congregation. This can give everyone an opportunity to read aloud some of the material included in worship.

Look at your own church or synagogue bulletins. Many have meaningful or symbolic covers. Encourage your students to bring any material used in their places of worship.

Here is a recent bulletin cover from my own church:

I
want you
to share your
Bread
with the
hungry,
open your homes
to the homeless
poor,
remove the
yoke of
injustice,
let the
oppressed go
free.

Isaiah: 58

Meaningful resources and activities are endless. Once you've started teaching you'll be on the lookout for teaching opportunities and applicable materials. Keep searching and be creative!

Let all things be done
decently and in order.

I Corinthians 14:40
(King James Version)

LESSON PLANNING, GOAL SETTING, EVALUATIONS

n order to make the most of the limited time you have with your students, it is important to plan your lessons well. Even with the best intentions, circumstances arise where adjustments must be made. Try to keep to the outline of your lesson plan, but always be ready to adapt to the needs of your students.

Suggested lesson formats for both one-hour or two-hour sessions could include the following:

SUGGESTED ONE-HOUR LESSON FORMAT
(USUALLY ONE-TO ONE)

<u>Time</u>	<u>Activity</u>
5 min.	Greetings and catch-up conversations.
10-15 min.	Review of home practice,written work and quick review of last session work, noting how materials were used. What worked best? Where were problems?
10 min.	Introduce new material, explaining purpose, encouraging student to discuss, question.
25 min.	Have student work on new material — reading, writing, etc.
5 min.	Student questions, assign home practice.
<u>5 min.</u>	Tutor reads aloud an inspirational piece.
60 min.	

SUGGESTED TWO-HOUR LESSON FORMAT
(USUALLY SMALL GROUPS)

Time	Activity
5 min.	Greetings and catch-up conversations.
10 min.	Review of home practice written work and quick review of last session work, noting how materials were used. What worked best? Where were problems?
10 min.	Introduce new material, explaining purpose, encouraging students ot discuss, question.
15 min.	Have students work on new material — reading, writing, etc.
20 min.	Give individuals an opportunity to work independently. Some students can write up first drafts of selected topics (parables, Bible stories, personal stories, words to hymns, etc.) Tutor can help individuals who need more basic help in specific skills, i.e., phonics, patterned words, alphabetizing, etc.
5 min.	BREAK
15 min.	Students read aloud stories that were written.
10 min.	Discussion.
20 min.	Students edit, rewrite stories. They can work in pairs or individually.
5 min.	Student questions, assign home practice.
5 min.	Tutor reads aloud an inspirational piece.
120 min.	

In order to focus your lessons on your students' goals, you must know what those goals are, both long-range and short-range.

A long-range goal might be "to read the Bible better," whereas a short-range goal could be to "read the chapter about 'love' in Corinthians." It is often more difficult for students to pinpoint short-term goals, but you can encourage them to state or write down specific things they want to do.

As we discussed individual goals in my small group, I suggested that they write them down.

Leola wrote:

> Read and writ BiBe Store
>
> Read and write lettle

Ruth wrote:

> Learn more about the Bible
> to become friends
> Write Stories about the Bible
> become more closer to Christ

Martha wrote in cursive:

> Reading and Writing better the story
> of the Bible. Spelling how to say thing
> and write them in the pro- Manner
>
> my life Story for me and my kids

Already they were zeroing in on what they wanted, but even at that first lesson I could assess some of their needs.

Objectives are the things that must be done to achieve the goal, the skills needed. In order to read the chapter about "love" in Corinthians, the objectives might be:

- Find Corinthians in the Bible
- Locate the "love" chapter and verses

- Read aloud the passage, even though hesitantly
- Discuss its meaning
- Write the most meaningful verses
- Learn new words, both for reading and writing

As you and your students identify these objectives, you can start planning lessons to incorporate reaching these objectives.

LESSON PLANS

Your Lesson Plan sheet can be as simple as writing down your plans for the lesson on the left side of a sheet of paper, leaving the right half free for comments and notes. You may want to identify some specific objectives you have in mind. Then, as the lesson progresses, quickly note or check off what was done on the right half of the page.

Writing up what happened in a previous lesson helps you plan realistically for the next lesson. It also reminds you what materials and books you want to bring.

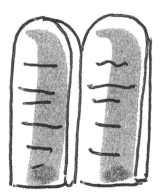

Be sure to look at your students' home practice work. It is discouraging if they have worked hard on a paper and no one asks to see it. Positive comments encourage students to try harder, and suggestions are easier to take after a comment such as, *Nicely done!* or *I can see you really worked hard on this!* Don't gush or say things that are obviously untrue, such as *Perfect!*, for most of us know we have a long way to go to be perfect. In the appendix is a list of "100 Ways to Say 'Very Good.'"

Assessment is constant and ongoing. Listen to your students—are their needs being met? Be aware that you are assessing each individual student's strengths and needs as you interact.

As learners read aloud, you can note who reads word by word, who stumbles over certain words, or who reads with meaning even though hesitantly. You can easily assess needs from both their reading and their writing. Keeping a portfolio of individual student writings allows you to review the work with each student. It also serves as a record to show where progress was made and areas where more help is needed. Learning individual student's needs can help as you individualize your lessons. More formal assessments can be made, with pre- and post-testing, by using such tools as LVA's *READ, Reading Evaluation-Adult Diagnosis.*[14]

Allow some time at the end of each session for you to read aloud an inspirational story or poem. This gives the students a time to relax. In doing so, they can experience the joy of listening to something being read without any tensions or responsibilities. *Guideposts Magazine* has many inspirational stories, as do church magazines and daily reading booklets.

For a small group, a meaningful way to end sessions together could be by forming a circle, holding hands, a quiet time. You might find this a symbolic way to show support and need for support. Each person holds the palm of the left hand *up*, the palm of the right hand *down*, as you connect and hold hands. This could signify that you are supporting the person on your left and being supported by the person on your right. This sounds easy, but it takes practice. If someone forgets, and they will, don't worry. The idea is to symbolize our support for one another. A squeeze passed along could be the sign for the end of the session.

Each tutor's lesson plans will differ depending on the students' abilities and needs. The ideas in Chapter 6, *Resources and Activities for Lessons*, can be used, but be as creative as you and your students want. You might want to review Chapter 5, *The First Meeting*, to note some of the suggestions given.

CASE HISTORIES

Before you start lessons with your own students, you might want to try making lesson plans for specific students. Here are four case histories, true to life, the kinds of people who could be assigned to you. Jot down ideas and plans that come to mind as you read each one. Then go back through this book to see if you can add more suggestions.

Case History #1

Marjorie sings in her church choir. She wants help in reading because she has to listen as the other choir members read new words and new music. She tries to memorize the words. She wishes she could read the words to new hymns herself.

Marjorie is a low-level reader—approximately 4th grade. She would like to write words to music; words and poetry are "in her head," she says, but she feels she cannot write the words.

How could you help her?

Case History #2

Joseph is a deacon in his small church. He knows many of the stories in the Bible, and sometimes is asked to tell the stories to the children. His pastor often asks him to read passages from the Bible before the congregation. He always makes excuses because he has trouble reading (low level—approximately 2nd grade). Because he reads word by word, he loses his concentration, finding comprehension difficult.

Joseph would like help in finding known passages in the Bible as well as reading them. He'd like to write the stories he knows, for he sometimes forgets them and would like them down on paper.

How could you help him?

Case History #3

Louise is active in her church, an usher, a leader of the missionary society. She has been asked to help write the bulletin for her church, but had to make excuses, for she feels she can't write. Her missionary group gets letters from a sister group in Africa that they help. She wishes she could read the letters. She must wait until the next society meeting when she asks another member to read it aloud to the group. She'd like to write back to them, but she feels that this is impossible.

Louise went to the 9th grade but reads at approximately the 3rd grade level.

How could you help her?

Case History #4

Natalia, a Russian Jew, came to America several years ago. She speaks and understands English fairly well, has many friends, and is active in the women's group in her synagogue. She is embarrassed because she cannot read or write English. So far, none of her friends knows her secret. She wants desperately to be able to read and write English, for she wants to join a study group in her synagogue where they are studying the Hebrew Bible.

Natalia only went to the 5th grade in Russia but can read and write Russian adequately. She reads and writes no English.

How could you help her?

<u>Small Group Case History</u>

Now jot down some suggestions for lesson plans if these four were in your small group. What would you have them do separately? What could they do together?

Making lesson plans for these real-life students will help you realize how you *can* adapt the techniques and suggestions given to any students. Careful planning, willingness to adjust and adapt, and common sense make for effective teaching.

Let us not be
weary in well doing;
for in due season
we shall reap,
if we faint not.

Galatians 6:9
(King James Version)

THE NEXT STEPS

*H*ow long you work with your student or small group depends on all of you. You always have choices: You can continue to the end of your contracted period, feeling you have accomplished whatever goals you and the learners set; or you can decide to continue for another contracted period.

Both of our small groups elected to work for a second period, and even further. Leola wanted to stay with our group, for we had become friends. Everyone gained a sense of trust and felt free to share as we learned. Gaining self-understanding, Leola also realized that she needed special help and asked to have one-to-one tutoring. In the men's small group, Freeman requested similar extra help.

EXTENDING THE SKILLS LEARNED

Martha saw other applications of skills we had used in our small group in studying the Bible. One day, Martha quietly asked if I would help her write a report to her boss. He wanted her to record all she had done to help neighborhood women in the place where she worked. I suggested to Martha that we do just as we did with our Bible stories: brainstorm, write down key words, and write up the report. Martha wrote, revised, rewrote, edited, and rewrote. This is what she finally came up with:

REPORT TO THE RESCUE MISSION PEOPLE

For the past four years I have tried to get parent participation at the Center,

1. By having a fellowship meeting
2. By having a craft and sewing club
3. By having a Bible club about prayer at home
4. By having Clothing Distribution Center (CDC) trips where people can get used clothes

5. By inviting Mrs. Colvin of Literacy Volunteers to give lessons in reading and writing Bible materials
6. By having a luncheon where I showed them how to prepare free foods given by the Rescue Mission
7. By offering transportation for grocery shopping
8. By taking them to Brighton Family Center for workshops
9. By taking them on family outings
10. By offering to take them to school activities

This report was instrumental in getting Martha a pay raise.

EXTENDING THE SKILLS TO HELP IN PERSONAL LIVES

Ruth was having a difficult time at home, with many personal and family problems. I suggested that she might want to write about some of her feelings; it might help her to put it on paper, and perhaps it might some day help someone else who was having similar problems. At the next session, Ruth slipped me a paper with this writing on it.

FAITH, HOPE, LOVE

Faith is some thing we all should have even when things seem at it worse Faith is believing that Christ will keep his promises of being right by our side through the good times And the bad times too, we all should Hope for a better day And hope for the security of God's Love For us with out Fear of the future we Love God because he loves us with forgiving And patient Love. the Truth is we live by God's word And his promises of his being there when we need him. when times are bad he watches over us more, His love is more powerful than Any other. He will Always be there for us no matter what.

It was a touching paper. The depth of Ruth's feelings and faith were coming out in her writing—things she never could say. And we talked about these words, *faith*, *hope* and *love*, how they could be nouns, or that *hope* and *love* could be action verbs. They liked the words best as action verbs.

EXTENDING THE SKILLS LEARNED TO OTHER AREAS OF LIFE

As my students picked up and sharpened their skills in reading and writing within the biblical context, I wondered if they would be interested in applying them to other areas of their lives.

In my men's group, we had talked about the genealogy of King David, of Abraham, and of Jesus. They had talked of James and John, brothers who had left their father and fishing nets to become "fishers of men." Would they be interested in their own genealogy? Keeping a record of their own families? They agreed to try.

My Family Tree

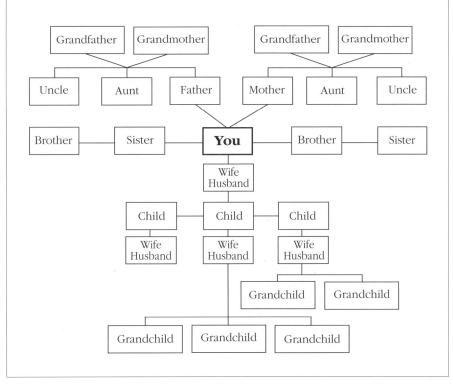

I had a simple Family Tree charted out and gave each student a copy. (See Appendix.) Each man wrote his own name and birth date in the center box. Connected to each side they added more boxes for names and birth dates of brothers and sisters.

They continued adding more boxes and more names—wife, date of marriage, children, dates of births, and grandchildren. Then they went to the upper level, adding father, mother, grandfather, grandmother.

By this time, the men were excited. They admitted they did not know certain dates but remembered they were in their home Bible; how did you spell this name? There were lines and boxes all over the page. James said he wanted to make a big chart and leave it on the kitchen table so that his children and grandchildren could include their own names and birth dates. After it was finished, he knew he would frame it. He also knew that his wife would want to make her family tree too, for she would want her children to know of her parents and grandparents as well.

Putting the unfinished family trees aside, I suggested each write his own name, just the first name, and think of himself as a small boy. Where was he born? One was born in a tiny town in Mississippi, another in a big city in North Carolina. Did their children know this? Probably not. I suggested that they think of something they did as small boys. Sam remembered making a slingshot and a scooter. James remembered going to a one-room school only for blacks. They recalled a favorite teacher, a fun game—ideas exploded, and they jotted down key words. Each man chose one story, and they began to write. The two-hour session had flown by, and both men put their papers away, still talking of boyhood memories.

The men and women in our small groups wanted to continue to work on reading biblical material. They wanted to do more writing on Bible stories. But they realized that the skills they had learned were transferable to other areas of their lives. The choice was theirs.

ENDINGS

Whether it is the end of a lesson or the end of your sessions together, it is a time for reflection. It is important to spend the last five or ten minutes *reading for pleasure*. There are many inspirational stories from religious magazines, from daily devotions. Giving the learners an opportunity to relax, to be inspired, sends them off with a positive thought no matter how difficult a lesson might have been.

If you and your students have decided to end the sessions together, acknowledge and affirm this decision. You might want to bring doughnuts and coffee; you might want to meet for lunch or breakfast.

The small group of women decided to have a picnic, bringing our families. We knew our formal meetings were at an end, but we also knew that we had found ourselves developing into a mutually caring group. We agreed that they could continue to call me, as I would call them, for support and encouragement.

As a parting gift, I gave each a tiny gold-plated cross to wear on their blouses or jacket collars. I wear mine, too, with pride, as a reminder of our small group, where together we focused on reading the Bible but found friendship as well.

The two men, Sam (who improved 2 reading levels) and Joe (who improved 3 reading levels), continued in my second small group. They wanted to end our sessions by sharing their work with members of their congregation. Standing in front of the church, they read their own writings on biblical topcis with pride. A tiny "cross in the pocket" is our reminder of our work together and our friendship.

Whether you teach one-to-one or in a small group, you can use the Bible and biblical stories and teachings as reading material *if*—and it's a big *IF*—your students want and have asked for it. It is most important that reading the Bible is your *students'* goal, not yours. But you can help them learn to read it for themselves.

MAKING A DIFFERENCE

Sometimes we, as volunteer tutors, feel that we may not have accomplished much. A lesson may have had to be repeated, for your students may not have remembered it. We sometimes feel that there is no big dramatic change in our students' lives. Is it all worthwhile?

May I paraphrase from a recent sermon I heard:

Sometimes small things are all that is possible. We must realize that not all our students will make those big and happy leaps forward. Not all soil is so rich that it will produce good crops. Not every group will produce genius students. Often we must be satisfied with little gains, but when you're the recipient of those small gains, it *is* important.

Little things mean a lot. Look to your own marriage or relationship with a special person. Would you prefer a big bash every five years or would you prefer a *thank you* with loving words each day? Think of your work. Would you prefer a retirement party and a gold watch after 25 years, or would you like a pleasant work relationship throughout the years? Your students, too, might prefer the little things that help them weekly, rather than some big reward at the end.

Little things add up. Remember the story of the tortoise and the hare? The plodding tortoise not only caught up to the fast running hare, but he quietly passed him by. Most of us realize that we cannot change the whole world, but we must remember that we *can* help one person, we *can* make a difference, we just might be able to change a part of the world. Few of us will have opportunities to make big changes in the world, but all of us have opportunities to change individual lives. By teaching one person to read and write, by helping that person read what he or she wants to read, the Bible, you are indeed a part of that bigger world.[15]

> Like all good teachers,
>   the world repeats her lesson.
> Over and over
> ...with wordless variety...
>   she spells the name of Love.
>
> — *Joan Walsh Anglund* [16]

Endnotes

1. Cheatham, Judy Blankenship, Ruth Johnson Colvin and Lester L. Laminack, *TUTOR: A Collaborative Approach to Literacy Instruction.* (Literacy Volunteers of America, Inc., 1993), pp. 22-24. Available from LVA (Order #91088), 800-LVA-8812.

2. Tibbets, Christine, "You Can Help LVA Tifton Tift County," LVA Tifton Tift County, GA, Newsletter, Vol. 1, No. 1, Fall 1989.

3. Anecdote provided by Dorothy Bush, LVA Tutor, LVA Troup County, GA.

4. *TUTOR*, pp. 25-30.

5. See Note 1.

6. *The Bible for Students* (Wheaton, IL: Tyndale House, 1990). Available from LVA (Order #60113), 800-LVA-8812.

7. Laminack, Lester L., *Reading With Children* (Literacy Volunteers of America, Inc., 1989). Available from LVA (Order #49001), 800-LVA-8812. Complete Training Module (Video with Ruth J. Colvin/Leader's Guide/*Reading With Children*, Order #49000) also available.

8. Colvin, Ruth J. and Jane Root, *Reading Evaluation Adult Diagnosis—READ* (Literacy Volunteers of America, Inc., 1982). Available from LVA (Order #91002) 800-LVA-8812.

9. See Note 1

10. *TUTOR*, pp. 53-56.

11. *TUTOR*, pp. 58-64.

12. *TUTOR*, pp. 66-73.

13. *TUTOR*, pp. 79-85.

14. See Note 8.

15. From a sermon by Rev. Ted Taylor, DeWitt Community Church, Syracuse, NY.

16. Anglund, Joan Walsh, *A Cup of Sun* (New York: Harcourt, Brace, Jovanovich, Inc., 1967) p. 17.

APPENDIX

- Resources
- Student/Tutor Agreement
- Read/Write Time Sheet
- Fry Readability Chart/Directions
- Manuscript/Cursive Writing
- Suggested Key words - Phonics, biblical context (sample)
- Alphabetizing Exercise Sheets
  Books of the New Testament
  Books of the Hebrew Scriptures
  People in the Bible
- Sample exercise sheets—capitals, punctuation, etc.
- Family Tree Master
- 100 ways to say "Very Good"

Resources

For Tutors

The Bible for Students (1990). Wheaton, IL: Tyndale House. (Available through LVA.)

Cheatham, J.B., Colvin, R.J., and Laminack, L.L. (1993). *TUTOR: A Collaborative Approach to Literacy Instruction*. Syracuse, NY: Literacy Volunteers of America, Inc.

Cheatham, J., and Lawson, V.K. (1990). *Small Group Tutoring: A Collaborative Approach for Literacy Instruction*. Syracuse, NY: Literacy Volunteers of America, Inc.

Colvin, R.J., and Root, J. (1982) *Reading Evaluation Adult Diagnosis*. Syracuse, NY: Literacy Volunteers of America, Inc.

For Students

The Bible for Beginning Readers (1993). Nashville, TN: Thomas Nelson.

Bible for Today's Family: New Testament (1992). New York, NY: American Bible Society.

Bible Readings for Life: Favorite Stories and Verses From the Bible (1990). Wheaton, IL: Tyndale House. (Available through LVA.)

Biblical Posters and Postcards in African Settings, Life of Jesus Mafa, 24 rue du Marechal-Joffre, 78000 Versailles, France.

Good News Bible (1992). New York, NY: American Bible Society.

Good News For Modern Man (1966). New York, NY: American Bible Society. (New Testament)

Good News for New Readers, Series A and B. New York, NY: American Bible Society.

Holy Bible: Gospel of Mark (1990). Wheaton, IL: Tyndale House. (Available through LVA.)

Penner, L. (1992). *Bible Terms Made Easy*. Yreka, CA: New Words Digest.

Penner, L. (1992). *Favorite Psalms*. Yreka, CA: New Words Digest.

Penner, L. (1992). *Make It Simple, Please: How to Simplify the Bible*. Yreka, CA: New Words Digest.

Selected Books of the Bible, simplified. Yreka, CA: New Words Digest.

Literacy Volunteers of America, Inc.
Student/Tutor Agreement

For a period of _____ weeks, from _____ to _____

Tutor agrees to:

_____

_____

_____

_____

_____

_____

Student agrees to:

_____

_____

_____

_____

_____

_____

Date _____   Tutor _____

                             Student _____

This form may be copied.

Literacy Volunteers of America, Inc.
Read/Write Time Sheet

Name .... Date ....

I will read or write at least 15 minutes each day for at least 5 days a week for 4 weeks starting: ....

Time of Study

Dates -- Week of	Monday	Tuesday	Wednesday	Thursday	Friday	Saturday	Sunday

This form may be copied.

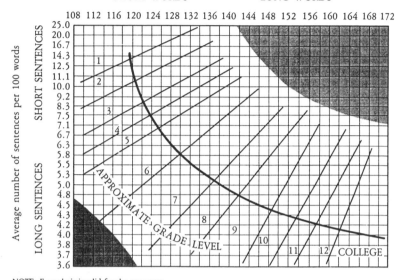

Average number of syllables per 100 words

SHORT WORDS   LONG WORDS

NOTE: Formula is invalid for the gray areas.

Procedure: 1. Choose three 100-word selections, one from the beginning, one from the middle, and one from the end of the text.
2. Count and average the number of syllables per 100 words.
3. Count and average the sentences per 100 words.
4. Apply the results of steps 2 and 3 to the graph.

SOURCE: Fry, E. *Reading Instruction for Classroom and Clinic*. Copyright © 1972 by McGraw-Hill, Inc. Used with the permission of McGraw-Hill Book Company.

D'Nealian alphabets From SCOTTFORESMAN, D'NEALIAN® HANDWRITING, Book 4 by Donald Neal Thurber, Copyright© 1993 by Scott Foresman and Company. Reprinted by permission.

Literacy Volunteers of America, Inc.
Suggested Key Words for
Teaching Phonics

b - Bible, baby, Bethlehem, book, born-again, baptism

c - cross, camel, confess, communion, cathedral

d - disciple, dove, doctrine

f - fish, fisherman

g - God, gods, giving, gospel

h - hallelujah, hell, heaven, holy

j - judge, Jehovah, justified, justice

k - king, kingdom

l - lamb, law, Lord, love, lectern

m - manna, meek, Messiah, Moses, minister, mass

n - neighbor, New Testament, Noah

p - Passover, pastor, preacher, praise, pews, pulpit, prayer

r - rabbi, religion, redeem, repent, righteous

s - sin, salvation, sanctify, songs, sermon, sacrament, sabbath, sanctuary, savior

t - temple, temptation, Ten Commandments, tithe, testimony, Torah, tabernacle

v - virgin, vision, vow

w - wisemen, worship, word, witness

y - yoke

z - zeal, Zion

ch - church, chancel

sh - sheep, shepherds

th - thresh

qu - quench

/k/ sound - ch - Christ, Christmas, Christian, choir

/s/ sound - ps - psalm

This form may be copied.

Literacy Volunteers of America, Inc.
Alphabetizing Exercise Sheet

Purpose: To practice alphabetizing skills

Directions: Put the books of the New Testament in alphabetical order, using the first letter or the second/third letters when necessary. Put (1) before the name that comes first alphabetically, then (2), (3), etc. Or you may find it easier for beginning students if names are put on 3 x 5 cards, asking them to put the cards in alphabetical order.

Example: (3) Saul
   (1) Daniel
   (2) Moses

Matthew	1 Timothy
Mark	2 Timothy
Luke	Titus
John	Philemon
Acts of the Apostles	Hebrews
Romans	James
1 Corinthians	1 Peter
2 Corinthians	2 Peter
Galatians	1 John
Ephesians	2 John
Philippians	3 John
Colossians	Jude
1 Thessalonians	Revelation
2 Thessalonians	

This form may be copied.

Literacy Volunteers of America, Inc.
Alphabetizing Exercise Sheet

Purpose: To practice alphabetizing skills.

Directions: Put the books of the Hebrew Scriptures in alphabetical order, using not only the first letter but the second and third letters when necessary. Put (1) before the name that comes first alphabetically, then (2), (3), etc. Or you may find it easier for beginning students if names of books are put on 3 x 5 cards, asking them to put the cards in alphabetical order.

Example: (3) Malachi
(1) Jeremiah
(2) Joshua

Genesis	Proverbs
Exodus	Ecclesiastes
Leviticus	Song of Solomon
Numbers	Isaiah
Deuteronomy	Jeremiah
Joshua	Lamentations
Judges	Ezekiel
Ruth	Daniel
1 Samuel	Hosea
2 Samuel	Joel
1 Kings	Amos
2 Kings	Obadiah
1 Chronicles	Jonah
2 Chronicles	Micah
Ezra	Nahum
Nehemiah	Habakkuk
Esther	Haggai
Job	Zachariah
Psalms	Malachi

Literacy Volunteers of America, Inc.
Alphabetizing Exercise Sheet

Purpose: To practice alphabetizing skills

Directions: Put the following biblical names in alphabetical order, using not only the first letter of each name but the second and third letters when necessary. Put (1) before the name that would be first in alphabetical order, then (2), (3), etc. Or you may find it easier for beginning students if names of books are put on 3 x 5 cards, asking them to put the cards in alphabetical order.

Example: (3) Titus
        (1) Jonah
        (2) Judas

A-J	K-Z
Job	Saul
Jesus	Peter
Isaiah	Martha
Adam	Sarah
Hosea	Mary
Eve	Moses
Judas	Samuel
Benjamin	Zebedee
Joseph	Miriam
Jonah	Timothy
Daniel	Paul
Jacob	Zachariah
James	Samson
Elijah	Ruth
Joshua	Thomas
John	Titus
Abraham	Simon
David	Pilate
Elizabeth	Mark

This form may be copied.

90

Literacy Volunteers of America, Inc.
Exercise Sheet
Capitals, Periods, Question Marks, Quotation Marks

Purpose: To put in appropriate capitals, periods, question marks and quotation marks.

Directions: - In exercise 1, write a capital letter over the lower case letter when appropriate, adding periods and question marks. In exercise 2, also include appropriate quotation marks.

Sample:

1   god talked to moses on the mountain was moses afraid
     God talked to Moses on the mountain. Was Moses afraid?

2   don't be afraid, moses, said god
     "Don't be afraid, Moses," said God.

Exercise 1 -

moses heard god speaking
david was a king
daniel was put in a lion's den
psalms are songs and prayers
job taught us about suffering
god said we should honor our parents
mary was afraid when she first saw the angel
john told the people about jesus
jesus said that the man was good
jesus said that we should love one another

Exercise 2 -

the 23rd psalm says, the lord is my shepherd
god said, you shall have no other gods before me
mary said, jesus is my baby
jesus said, i am the way
john said, there is one greater than i
jesus said, come unto me
love one another, said jesus
honor thy father and thy mother, god said in the ten commandments
why have you forsaken me jesus said

My Family Tree

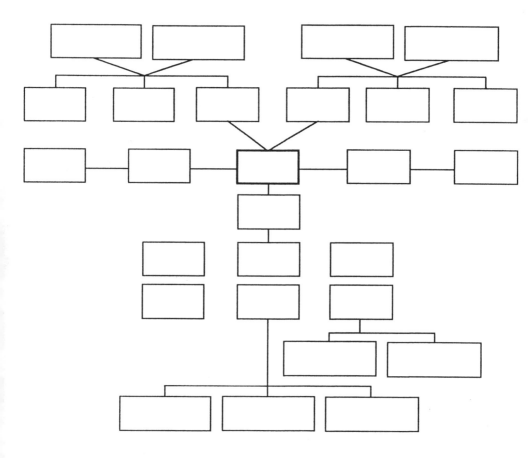

100 Ways to Say "Very Good"

1. You're right
2. Good Work!
3. Well done.
4. You did a lot of work today!
5. It's a pleasure to work with you.
6. Now you have it.
7. Fine job!
8. That's right!
9. Neat!
10. Super!
11. Nice going.
12. That's coming along nicely.
13. That's great!
14. You did it that time!
15. Fantastic!
16. Terrific!
17. Good for you!
18. Make it so!
19. That's better.
20. Excellent!
21. Good job (name).
22. Superfine!
23. That's good.
24. Good going.
25. That's really nice.
26. WOW!
27. Keep up the good work.
28. Outstanding!
29. Fantastic!
30. Good for you!
31. What talent!
32. Good thinking.
33. Exactly right!
34. You make it look easy.
35. Yes!
36. Awesome!
37. Way to go.
38. Superb!
39. OK!
40. You're on target.
41. I knew you could do it.
42. Wonderful!
43. You're great.
44. Beautiful work.
45. You've worked hard on this!
46. That's the way.
47. Keep trying.
48. That's it.
49. Let's tell the boss.
50. You're very good at that.
51. You're learning fast.
52. You certainly did well today.
53. I'm glad your approach is working
54. Keep it up!
55. I'm proud of you.
56. That's the way.
57. You're learning a lot.
58. That's better than ever.
59. Quite nice.
60. You've figured it all out.
61. Perfect!
62. Fine!
63. I'll sign the order.
64. You've got it.
65. You figured that out fast.
66. Very resourceful.
67. You are really improving.
68. Look at you go.
69. You've really got that down pat.
70. Tremendous!
71. I like that.
72. I couldn't do it better myself.
73. Now that is what I call a fine job.
74. You did that very well.
75. Impressive!
76. Sharp!
77. Right on!
78. That's wonderful.
79. You mastered that in no time.
80. Very nice.
81. Congratulations.
82. That was first class work.
83. Sensational.
84. You don't miss a thing.
85. You make our work fun.
86. You must have been practicing it.
87. I'm glad I assigned this to you.
88. You came through again.
89. DYNAMITE!
90. I knew I could count on you.
91. You deserve a raise.
92. How can I help you with this?
93. Go for it!
94. The Best!
95. You have my complete support.
96. MARVELOUS!
97. Clever idea.
98. I'm glad you are on our team.
99. You're really on the ball.
100. Thank you!

© 1992 by Roger L. Firestien, Ph.D., Center for Studies in Creativity, P.O. Box 615, Williamsville, NY 14231.